b small publishing

TERRIBLE TRICKS
AND
DEVIOUS DISGUISES

Susan Martineau

Illustrations by Martin Ursell

Published by small publishing ltd, The Book Shed, 36 Leyborne Park, Kew, Richmond, Surrey, TW9 3HA, UK

© b small publishing, 2002

5 4 3

Colour reproduction: Vimnice International Ltd., Hong Kong.   Printed in China by WKT Co. Ltd.
Editorial: Susan Martineau *Design:* Louise Millar *Production:* Catherine Bruzzone and Madeleine Ehm
ISBN 978-1-902915-63-0
British Library Cataloguing-in-Publication Data. A catalogue record for this book is available from the British Library.

Before You Begin

You'll probably already have most of the things you
need for these tricks and disguises around the house.

empty matchboxes

elastic bands

sticky tape

rope

newspapers

For great disguises you could start collecting cast-off jackets, old glasses and sunglasses, hats, scarves and so on. Jumble sales and charity shops are brilliant places to find things too.

wool

felt-tip pens

cottonwool

Practise your tricks before doing them for your friends and family. You could wear a special disguise for your shows. When you are ready to perform remember you don't want your audience too close. It's also best not to play the practical jokes on anyone of a nervous disposition!

old make-up

paper and card

You will need a bit of grown-up help in one or two places. These have been marked with this special symbol.

!

Matchbox Magic

Cunning Coin Trick

You'll really confuse your friends and family with this nifty trick. You'll need to be wearing a long-sleeved shirt or sweatshirt to perform it.

What you will need:
- 4 identical empty matchboxes
- some coins
- sticky tape

Place the coins in one matchbox. Push it up your right sleeve so it will be out of sight. Tape it to your wrist.

Place the other 3 empty boxes on the table. Ask your friends to gather round.

Using your left hand, pick up 2 of the boxes in turn. Shake them. They will sound empty.

Fastest Wand in the World

The fastest magician in the world is Eldon D. Wigton, also known as Dr Eldoonie. On 21 April 1991 he performed 225 different tricks in 2 minutes. Keep practising!

Pick up the third box with your right hand and shake it. The coins up your sleeve will rattle. Move the boxes around. (Only move them using your left hand!) Ask a friend to tell you which one has the coins in it. Hmmm, tricky eh?

The Moving Matchbox

This is a simple but rather creepy trick. At your command the matchbox on the back of your hand will sit up!

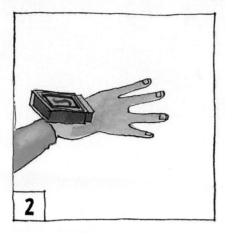

1

2

3

Pull the drawer of the matchbox a little way out. Squeeze the skin on the back of your hand.

Catch the skin between the drawer and the outer box. Close the drawer carefully to keep the skin trapped.

Keep your wrist straight and your hand open. The box will lie flat. Bend your wrist and close your hand. The box will sit up on end.

The Disappearing Magician

In 1939 William 'Doc' Nixon disappeared without a trace. This magician, who liked to appear in oriental costume, was never seen again!

5

Slap in the Face!

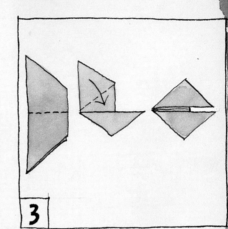

This trick has probably been a favourite of schoolchildren since paper was invented. Have a trusting friend standing by.

What you will need:
• a sheet of plain A4 paper

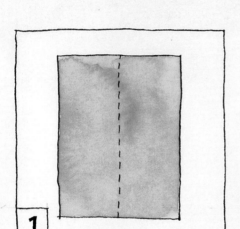

1 Fold the paper in half, lengthwise. Open it up again.

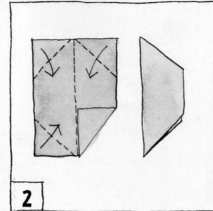

2 Fold in each corner to meet the fold in the middle. Fold the paper in half.

3 Make a crease in the middle. Fold both points down so the long edges meet the middle crease.

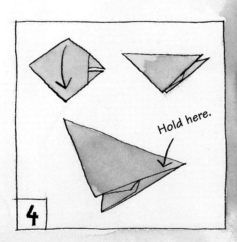

Hold here.

4 Turn the paper over. Fold the 2 points together.

Now you are ready for action! Hold the banger by its bottom points and whoosh it down sharply and quickly. At the same time pretend to slap your friend! Great sound effect, eh?

BANG!

Predictatrick

This is good fun and will mystify your friends. You need to be facing your audience.

What you will need:
- pencil or pen
- 8 small sheets of paper
- a hat or bag

1
Ask your friends to call out 8 different names or numbers. They could be their own names.

2
Make sure they cannot see what you are writing. Write only the first name or number that was called out on EVERY sheet.

3
Fold each sheet and place them in the hat or bag. Ask a friend to pick one out and then tell them what is written on the sheet. They will be amazed when they open it to check!

Spooky Prediction

In 1898, fourteen years before the sinking of the Titanic, a book called *The Wreck of the Titan* was published. It was the story of a vast ocean liner that hits an iceberg. Was the author, a man named Morgan Robertson, able to see into the future or was this just an eerie coincidence?

Headless Horror

You'll need a friend to help you with this horrible practical joke. (Please remember not to frighten your granny.) You also need to be wearing a pair of trousers or a skirt you can hitch up under your armpits.

What you will need:
- large piece of cardboard
- scissors
- sticky tape
- large piece of red fabric (an old T-shirt or towel)
- very large shirt
- large adult-sized jacket

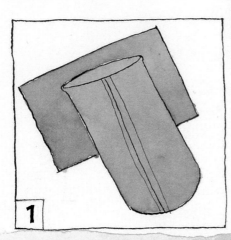

1 Curl the cardboard into a tube and tape it firmly.

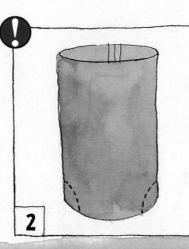

2 Cut the tube, as shown, so it will sit well on your shoulders.

3 Cut a hole for your head. Cover the top end with the fabric and tape it firmly.

The Headless Horseman

Beware the Dullahan! In Irish legend he is a terrifying headless horseman riding an awful black steed. He holds his head under his arm, the huge eyes staring. His face looks like mouldy cheese. If the Dullahan knocks on your door he'll throw a bucket of blood at you. The only thing he is afraid of is gold – and you can save yourself from certain death with a gold ring.

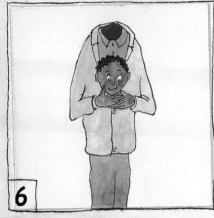

Hitch your trousers or skirt up. Get your friend to dress you in the shirt. Button it up around your head! Tuck it in.

Put the jacket on over the shirt. Put your arms through the sleeves. Do up the bottom of the jacket.

Hold your head in your hands and go in search of your first victim!

The Headless Earl

Thomas Percy, seventh Earl of Northumberland, was executed for treason by Elizabeth I of England. His head was put on a spike and his body was buried. It is said that the ghost of the Headless Earl can be seen stumbling about in search of his severed head!

! ! ! Terrible Tips ! ! !

You could paint your face white and gel your hair. Make a set of vampire fangs out of a piece of white plastic yogurt pot.

9

Crack 'Em if You Can!

Are you made of the right stuff to make a spy? Have you got what it takes to undertake a secret mission?

Holey Code

Pass a secret message to another agent hidden inside a newspaper.

Look at the date on the front of the newspaper. Choose a page inside the newspaper with the same page number as one of the numbers in the date. Using a pin, prick a hole over the letters in that page to spell out your message.

Prick a hole in the number in the date to let your partner know which page to find the message on.

When the holey page is held up to the light, they'll be able to spell out the message.

Secret Agent Jasper

A chap called Jasper Maskelyne performed in Cairo, Egypt during World War II as 'The Royal Command Magician'. He was, in fact, working for the British Intelligence Service as a spy!

Keyword Code

Choose a word or phrase in which letters are not repeated. Write the word or phrase in a column as shown. Then write the alphabet, leaving out any letters which have appeared already in the word or phrase. In a second column write the whole alphabet as normal. Spell out the messages using the first column.

Jowr ioqqseo bq bj khc rnoo.

means

Next message is in old tree.

Nifty Number Code

Choose a number and make sure all agents know what it is. For example, if your number is 7 the following pattern is to be used: A equals 7, B equals 8, C equals 9, D equals 10 and so on.

7.24.11 31.21.27. 15.20 10.7.20.13.11.24.? is code for: *Are you in danger?*

It's harder to decode if you don't leave spaces in between the words!

You can change the number if you suspect enemy agents are on the trail!

16.7.25.22.11.24 —
19.7.25.17.11.18.31.20.11 —
29.21.32 — 11.24.1

Identikit Puzzle

Match up the bits of face to blow the cover of three extremely dangerous agents.

See if you can spot the agents as they really are. They're somewhere in the book!

! ! ! Top Spy Tip ! ! !

A simple way to disguise your own handwriting is to write with your other hand. This is a bit tricky but your writing will not look like your own!

Make a Magic Wand

It's really easy to make your own magic wand. Then you can use it for all your tricks as well as the rather nasty one here!

What you will need:
- 16-cm length of wooden stick
- pencil
- masking tape

- black and white paints
- paintbrush
- dollop of plasticine or similar

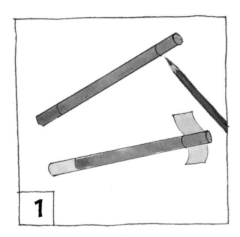

1

Make pencil marks 2 cm in from the ends of the stick. Wrap masking tape round the ends.

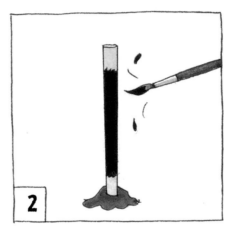

2

Paint the main part of the stick black. When it's dry remove the tape.

3

Paint the ends white and let them dry. Hey presto!

‼ Magic Tip ‼

Use the dollop of plasticine to hold the wand steady as you paint it.

Aargh . . . My leg!

This is a simple and horrid trick!
You might like to practise this in front of
a mirror before your performance.

What you will need:
- thick white paper
- scissors
- your magic wand
- glue

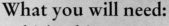

1

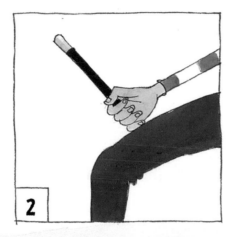

2

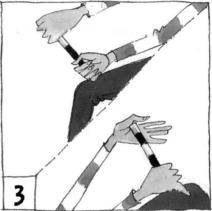

3

Cut a piece of paper 2 cm
wide. Roll it into a tube to
fit round the wand. Glue
the edge carefully.

Hold the wand as shown.
Hide the end on your leg
with one hand.

With the other hand
gradually push the tube
down the wand. Keep the
end of the wand hidden
behind your hand and
wrist. Ouch!

The Legless Trickster

Eliaser Bamberg was a court magician in
eighteenth-century Holland. He had lost a leg in
an accident and had a special artificial one
made with all kinds of compartments. He could
perform amazing tricks using this 'magical' limb!

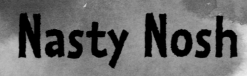

Nasty Nosh

Offer your friends a delightful snack! This is great for Hallowe'en parties or any dark and spooky night.

Eyeballs on the Rocks

Make these gory ice cubes the night before you want to use them.

What you will need:
- large radishes
- small black olives, stoned
- sharp knife
- ice-cube tray
- big jug of tomato juice

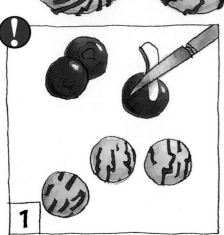

1 Peel the radishes, leaving a bit of red skin on them.

2 With the tip of the knife dig a small hole in each radish. Push an olive into each hole.

3 Pop the stuffed radishes into the slots of the ice-cube tray. Fill with water and freeze overnight.

4 Fill some glasses with tomato juice and pop a couple of eyeballs in each!

Toasted Tongues

What you will need to serve 2 people:

- 4 slices of bread, white or brown
- 2 slices of salami or ham
- scissors and a knife
- chopping board
- grill pan
- tomato ketchup

Use a chopping board.

1

2

3

Cut each slice of bread into a mouth shape using scissors. Cut 4 tongues out of the ham or salami.

Cut a slit between the lips using the knife. Pop a tongue into each mouth.

Place the mouths under the grill and toast lightly. Serve with the ketchup.

Vampires!

Stories about vampires have been around since Roman times. All over the world you can find legends about beings that drink human blood in order to live forever. There's a Chinese vampire with red eyes and green hair, a Malaysian one that trails its insides along behind it, and a Greek creature that is half woman, half snake.

The most famous vampire of all is Count Dracula from the book by Bram Stoker. The author based his character on a real-life count from Transylvania – known as Vlad the Impaler because of the blood-thirsty way he got rid of people he didn't like!

All Knotted Up

The Great Knot Challenge

Challenge your friends to tie a simple knot in a short piece of rope without letting go of the ends at all! Then show them how it's done.

What you will need:
• a piece of string or rope about 120 cm long

1 Place the rope or string in front of you. Fold your arms completely.

2 Pick up one end of the rope or string in each hand.

3 Unfold your arms and you've tied a knot! It's easy – when you know how.

Pull a Rope Through Your Neck!

Just kidding! You know you must never put ropes around your neck!

What you will need:
- a piece of rope about 120 cm long
- a rollneck T-shirt or top

1 Hold the rope in the middle with both hands. Then tuck the middle under the front of the rollneck.

2 The 2 ends should hang down in front of you. It now looks like the rope is round your neck. Of course it isn't!

3 Gather your audience. Tie the ends of the rope in a knot at your neck. Yank it fast and pull the rope away from you. EEEEEEURGH!

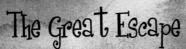

The Great Escape

Harry Houdini is one of the most famous magicians and escape artists ever. Audiences would suggest impossible places to escape from and Harry would do it! He could escape from padlocked crates thrown into rivers, giant paper bags without tearing them, and even a bronze coffin submerged in a swimming-pool. He died on Hallowe'en 1926 – spooky!

Old Before Your Years

Even your mother may not recognize you like this! The hideous headgear on page 20 looks really brilliant with this outfit. Why not add a moustache too (see page 21)?

The Anti-facelift

Screw up your eyes and see where the wrinkles appear. Open your eyes and use eyebrow pencil to draw along each crease. You'll age by decades!

Draw creases and wrinkles around your mouth and nose.

Draw bags under your eyes with the pencil too. Shade underneath for amazingly aged eyes. Make your eyebrows look shaggier by pencilling in some more bushy bits.

Half wolf, half man!

An old, old superstition says that there are certain people who can change into fearsome wolves. Scientists have looked into this belief and reckon there may be an illness that can make people really hairy and violent!

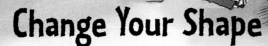

Change Your Shape

Wear your normal clothes. On top of them start adding padding.

1 Tie cushions round your waist using string or rope.

2 Wind scarves and small towels round your arms and legs.

3 Put a towel around your shoulders.

4 Wear clothes that are a few sizes too big over the top. Wear big shoes too.

5 Practise walking in a stooped way. Maybe add a walking stick to finish the disguise.

The Shape of Fashion

Strange and amazing shapes have often been the fashion. In sixteenth-century Spain it was really cool for men to pad the front of their jackets with a false pot belly! The extra stuffing was made from bits of material, wool or horsehair.

During the reign of Elizabeth I of England the fashion for women included a farthingale. This was a fat roll of cushioning worn around the hips to make dresses stick out. It was meant to show off the embroidery on the material.

Get Ahead

Bald as a Coot!

Try and get your hands on some old, unwanted make-up for this. You could also make this with cottonwool.

What you will need:
- newspaper
- old white rubber swimming cap
- pencil
- 14 x 3 cm strip of card
- PVA glue
- white or grey wool
- scissors
- eyebrow pencil
- cosmetic foundation cream

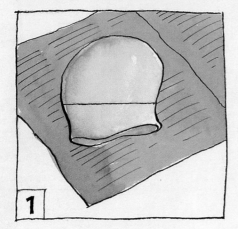

1 Cover your work surface with newspaper. Turn the cap inside out. Draw a line 5 cm up from the bottom.

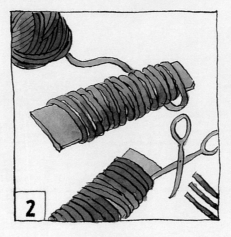

2 Wind lots of wool around the card. Cut the wool along one edge and lay out the strands.

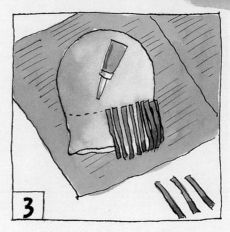

3 Glue along the line on the cap. Leave a gap of 4 cm at one end. Press strands on the glue. Leave to dry.

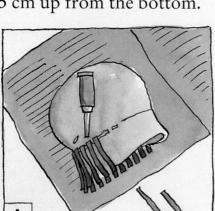
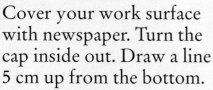

4 Turn the cap over and repeat. Don't forget to leave the 4-cm gap. Leave to dry.

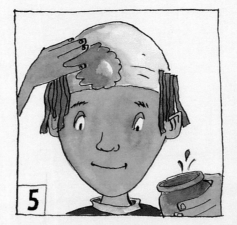

5 Pull the cap on. Cover the bald head with foundation cream to blend it in with your own skin.

6 Add wrinkles on the forehead using the eyebrow pencil. Trim the hair a bit if necessary.

Mighty Moustaches

You can make all kinds of amazing moustaches using the same basic method. You need some sticking plaster, wool and glue.

Draw the shape of the moustache on the plaster. Cut it out. Glue on strands of wool. Two layers looks good.

Peel the backing off the plaster and press it on to your face!

You could even make some bushy sideburns or eyebrows using the same technique. You'd be completely unrecognizable!

For a white moustache use cottonwool. Tie a piece of thread in the centre. Glue on 2 small bits of sticking plaster for fixing on to your face.

Scabby Pustules and Beastly Boils

Yuck! Yuck! Yuck! These delightful zits and buboes can be applied anywhere on your body. Make them as big as you like and experiment with different colours – brown for scabby, yellow and green for pus! Why not put some on the bald head on page 20 for a really disgusting disguise?

What you will need:
- washable felt-tips
- tissues
- PVA glue
- paintbrush

1 Tear off small bits of tissue. With felt-tips colour them yellow, red, brown or green or a mixture.

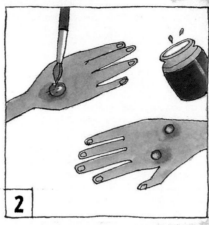

2 Scrunch up the tissue and place it on your skin. Brush some glue all over and around it. Let it dry.

Revolting Warts

Paint some latex (or art masking fluid) thickly on to a flat plastic lid. Let it dry and then roll it up as you peel it off the lid.

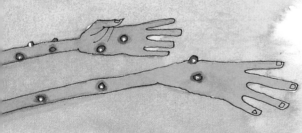

Black Death Buboes

During the fourteenth century millions of people were wiped out by a disease called the Black Death. Not only did your skin turn black but you got revolting lumps called buboes in your armpit and other parts of your body.

Colour with felt-tips. Glue a small piece of sticking plaster on the back of it and use this to fix it on to your skin.

Mega-sneeze Wheeze

This trick could also be called The Incredible Bouncing Bogey! It's a really simple joke with rather surprising results especially if you make a bit of Trick Snot to go with it.

What you will need:
- a small handkerchief or tissue
- a very bouncy rubber ball
- an elastic band

Trick Snot

Make a latex sausage (see the warts on page 22). Colour it green. Curl it into a ball and hold it close to your nose as you 'sneeze'. Watch your friends' faces as you unroll the 'snot' from your nose!

1

2

3

Place the ball in the centre of the hanky or tissue. Gather the hanky or tissue round it and put the elastic band around it tightly.

Put it all in your pocket and wait for a 'sneeze' to come along.

How does he do it?

Hold the hanky or tissue in both hands with the ball inside. As you 'sneeze' throw the whole lot on the ground in front of you.

The Bullet catch

Many magicians have died in the attempt to perform this most dangerous of tricks – to catch a bullet fired from a gun in their teeth or on a plate.

Most mysterious was the death of Chung Ling Soo in 1918. He died after trying the Bullet Catch and, after his death, it turned out he was not Chinese at all. He was an American called William E. Robinson.

Magic Banana Trick

Prepare this wacky trick and put it back in the fruit bowl. When someone wants a banana make sure you offer them this one!

What you will need:
- 1 banana
- a cocktail stick

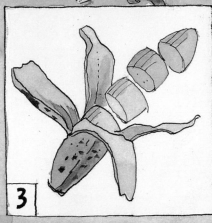

1 Push the stick into the banana carefully. Move it slowly from side to side, so that it slices the banana inside.

2 Repeat this a few times up the banana. The holes will look like speckles on the skin.

3 When it's peeled just watch your friends' faces.

Magic Circles

The Young Magicians' Club was formed in 1996 especially for people between the ages of 10 and 18. It's part of The Magic Circle – an organization for amateur and professional magicians with 1,500 members all over the world.

The International Brotherhood of Magicians is the largest magic society in the world with nearly 15,000 members. It also has a junior section called Magical Youth International.

They're the clubs to join if you're mad about magic!